Grapes From D'vine Fruit From Heaven

By
Donna Knight

Copyright ©2022
Donna Knight

All rights reserved. No part of this book may be used, reproduced, stored in a retrieval system or transmitted, in any form or by any means, including mechanical, electronic, photocopy, recording, scanning, and methods not invented or in common use at the time of this publication, without the prior written consent of the publisher and/or the author.

Scripture Reference – Unless otherwise stated all biblical references come from New King James Version Hebrew Greek Key Word Study Bible Copywrite by AMG International Inc. 1982 by Thomas Nelson Inc.

Printed in the United States of America

First Printing 2022

ISBN: 9798837448379

Dedication/Thank You

Dedicated to Our God, Jesus, and the Holy Spirit without whom none of this would be possible.

Deepest Gratitude to my husband, Quovadis King, who is willing to walk this path with me no matter what it looks like. God has used you to help me become a better woman, minister and wife. Thank you for hanging in here with me. Love you husband.

To my sister Delores Angela Knight, when you died you left a hole in my heart, that only God could fill. I will never be the same without you. I will be doing all I can to ensure I see you one day in heaven. My sister, Hilda, (Scrappy Doo), for loving and supporting me. To my mother Delores who even in this time of dementia has always been my biggest fan. Thank you God, for allowing her to continue to remember me. My niece Deanna for everything she is, has and continues to do, I love you more than you will ever know.

Special shout to Taraya Maxwell- for all her help with editing. I didn't know what it took. God provided. She was flawless, suggestive and professional. Find her on Facebook @FBAW the brand or Rayamaxw@yahoo.com

Also shout outs to Book Marketeers for their step-by-step help. You guys and gals are awesome.

Special Thanks to ALL of YOU who are reading and putting into action all that God has and is giving.

THANK YOU.

PREFACE

As the author, I am bringing you biblical truths through the work of the Holy Spirit in my life. I am an Ordained Minister. Don't let that fool you. As you read on the back cover, my life hasn't been easy. Within the reality of the things that have and will happen, God sent His Living Word to rescue me and keep me from falling. He WILL watch over His Word to perform it. *(Jeremiah 1:12)*

He gave me HIS PEACE even before I knew who He was. You are never alone in this world, especially once you realize the Great Creator, Our God is with you and always has been. You will feel Hope within these pages. A HOPE for a blessed tomorrow. You can do all things thru Christ who strengthens you. *(Philippians 4:13)*

You will hear of His Word being used in my world to pull me up and out of darkness. It will work in your world. The most important thing that I pray comes from this book is Love. Your self-love and knowledge that God, our True Living Creator, LOVES you. It doesn't matter what you have done, if you come to Him, He will receive, forgive and rebuild.

I have referenced issues in my life to be transparent in what we as believers go through. Big or small, God is with you. Each scripture, prayer, and reflection are Spirit-driven. I pray my transparency helps you as I have been helped.

I use Jesus, God, Christ, Jehovah, The Father, and Yeshua interchangeably. I won't argue about the name of God, His Son, or the Holy Spirit because they are one. Each is a functioning piece of the Triune God working seamlessly together for our sanctification and salvation. Neither is apart from the other. They are all powerful, all knowing and always present. God is the Alpha and Omega.

Just as I know there is a God, I also know there is an adversary. He has many names, faces and emotions. He is NOT all powerful. He does NOT get to run our lives and He MUST fall under the subjection of what the Word says in (1Peter 5:8); resist the devil and he must flee. Keep this in the forefront of your mind. It's your weapon of mass destruction.

Any reference to music, TV, or other reflective memories is purely for understanding. I don't own the rights to any person, place, or thing used by God in my life.

This devotional has scripture, prayer, reflections, and note pages. Use them.

Scripture is necessary; the Word has power. We need to meditate on the Word each week. What we work on will sink into our daily lives. It takes more than one attempt to try to get good at something. Make Scripture a daily routine.

Prayer will help you get closer to God. Use those I have supplied or add your own. The Father wants to hear from you. You must ask God to move in your life. Our God is a gentleman. Give Him permission to make you over in His Image. He will come in and change your heart.

Reflection is what you can learn about yourself. There may be other issues that come forth; trust the Holy Ghost to lead you to and through it all. Be honest with who you are, God already knows. Don't hide what needs to be healed.

Notes give you a place to write about whatever is revealed and release it from inside. Use extra paper if you need to. Letting it out, gives it to God to work on and you can get to living an abundant life. Once you let it go, don't go back and pick it up. Bare it, bury it and walk away.

This is a 52-week devotional. Whichever week you begin is the right time. Don't rush. Take each week and do the work. It doesn't take much to see results, but it does take effort on your part. A healthy habit comes when we begin to do the same good thing daily.

Reuse this book as needed. Revisit your prayers and growth. Watch God working in your life. Always share it with a friend. Salvation and Godly direction are always good things to give away. When you finish, gift your friend, a work associate, or anyone else with their own copy. What we get from God, we must share with our brothers and sisters. That is the life Jesus wants us to lead.

(Acts 3:6) Peter answered and said; "Silver and Gold have I none, but what I do have I give you. In the Name of Jesus Christ of Nazareth, rise and walk.

A child doesn't begin to write the first time they pick up a pencil. Be lenient with yourself. Be gentle. There is a learning curve, but the grading is on a Jesus curve.

If I pick a grape from this tree,

Lord, I pray you will be with me.

I want to walk and learn the truth.

Open my heart to receive your fruit.

Open my eyes to see your Grace.

Take my hand and show me your face.

~Donna Knight

TABLE OF CONTENTS

Week 1: Don't Look Back 10

Week 2: Ears to Hear 12

Week 3: Faith Is For Now 14

Week 4: Allow Time To Heal 16

Week 5: No Matter What 18

Week 6: You Are More 20

Week 7: Trying to Get It Right 22

Week 8: Who Do You Need Me To Be? 24

Week 9: Hand Them Off 26

Week 10: A Friend Indeed 28

Week 11: Be Still 30

Week 12: God Has His Eyes On You 32

Week 13: The Lessons Are On-Going 34

Week 14: How To Capture Your Thoughts - A, B, C, And Always P 36

Week 15: Believe It 38

Week 16: Leave A Legacy 40

Week 17: I Just Want To Be Saved 42

Week 18: Always And In All Ways 44

Week 19: He Loves Me, He Loves Me Not 46

Week 20: Who Loves You Baby? 48

Week 21: The Exchange 50

Week 22: Action Vs. Reaction 52

Week 23: Renter Or Permanent Resident 54

Week 24: Help My Thoughts 56

Week 25: Thought Catcher 58

Week 26: Favor Is Yours 60

Week 27: Which Way Do I Go?... 62

Week 28: The Plan Has Already Been Made 64

Week 29: Holding My Tongue.. 66

Week 30: You're The Plan Maker; God Is The Way Maker 68

Week 31: God Is Working In Your Life 70

Week 32: Sustainable Living 72

Week 33: Will You Truly Believe?.. 74

Week 34: It's All In Your Mind 76

Week 35: Baby, I Got You Baby! 78

Week 36: Let's Get It Started 80

Week 37: He Never Said A Mumbling Word 82

Week 38: Aw Child, Shut Up! 84

Week 39: Mind-Changing Power 86

Week 40: I Believe 88

Week 41: It Isn't Getting Any Easier 90

Week 42: Under Contract 92

Week 43: He Is A Keeper 94

Week 44: Free Your Mind - The Rest Will Follow 96

Week 45: Overcomer 98

Week 46: I Will Be There To Hold Your Hand 100

Week 47: Hope To The Rescue 102

Week 48: You Have Angels 104

Week 49: The Offer Is Yours 106

Week 50: The Gift That Keeps On Giving 108

Week 51: Clean My Heart 110

Week 52: It Is Finished 112

The Final Word 114

Week 1: Don't Look Back

Daily we encounter many of life's unpleasantries. Instead of getting stuck in yesterday's hurts or mistakes, we need to look toward a promised future. There is always a new path that Christ is leading you toward. He says in His Word that He knows the paths you should take. Trust Him. Trust the process.

Looking back only brings reminders of things that were best left behind. It is called your past for a reason. There is no need to look back or drag your past like a boulder into your tomorrows. If you look back over your life, make sure it is only to see how far you've come.

Jesus came so we can get over our past and on to HIS Future. Today is the day we stop looking back and begin walking into our destinies. Begin to pursue His purpose for you. **I am not perfect, but I am saved.** You need to know that God, The Father, The Son, and The Holy Spirit live in you. Once you begin to trust this, you can get to the work at hand. There is so much more for you in your future.

This devotional is the first fruit of the *Grapes from D'Vine* series. Look for more to come. If you are reading this, know you and I will go forward together. Take one step today and trust God to lead you into HIS tomorrow. Believe that you are an essential part of God's plan.

Jeremiah 29:11 For I know the thoughts I think toward you, says the LORD, thoughts of peace and not of evil, to give you a future and a hope. (NKJV)

Prayer: Dear God, I am starting this journey with you right where I am. I believe you and I are working together with your Holy Spirit and the Word of God to accomplish miraculous changes in my life. I know I am not perfect, but with you, I am being perfected. I won't let the past dictate my future in you. Thank you for leading me. **AMEN**

Reflection: This week, look ahead. Write down where you see yourself in one year. What are your spiritual expectations?

Week 2: Ears to Hear

When trying to walk the right path, you need to hear directions clearly. While on the path, there will be distractions. There will be people's opinions, situational issues, death, job loss, and relational disputes.

The reason is, in states of confusion and stress, you are made spiritually and physically weak and incapable of fighting back or being rational. The devil wants you to be confused about if you really heard the voice of our God speaking or not. You won't have the strength to battle the accuser or hear from God.

The word says my sheep know my voice and listen. You will know God is giving you direction because He will show you how to apply the word to your life. This means you must read scripture, use it in your life and find His answers.

The word of God is full of very clear and specific instructions. Our lives are very complicated and unclear. The only way to make sense of it all, is through the Holy Spirit. It's not enough to know God's Word. We must "put it into practice." God shows you a Bible verse. You must use it and learn how to apply it to your specific situation. This is God giving you direction. Other signs may come through a Christian friend or physical signs. LOOK for the things that show you that you are doing HIS Will for your life.

I found, for me, the #3 is how He confirms in me. Look for your confirmation pattern. You are in Christ. He is confirming things in your life. Now go out and take care of what it is that you are being called to do.

Matthew 11:15 He who has ears, let him hear (NKJV)

Prayer: Father, don't just give me ears to hear; give me the heart to follow where your Word leads me. I want to be obedient to You and your will for my life. Confirm in me when it is your voice I hear and not the voice of a trickster, until I get used to listening. Help me separate the white noise from your guidance and listen with confidence as you speak to me. **AMEN**

.

Refection: What do you feel God is leading you to do? Why are you unsure that you can do it? This devotional is a look at what stepping out and believing in God looks like. Believe me, it's scary but have no fear. If God said it, He will bless it. Listen this week for guidance, big or small, God is leading you.

Week 3: Faith Is For Now

If you have never believed in anything in your life, it is time to take a stand. You must decide what side you are going to be on.

There is a worldly side that believes that there is no God and nothing worth living for. There is no happiness, no peace, and no HOPE. There is only hate, violence and despair. How dark and dismal is that, to live a life without any joy or vision for a future? That is how this world can make you feel due to the tricks of satan.

The good news is, as a restored child of God, there is a better outlook on the horizon. There is hope for peace that can only be found through a relationship with Yeshua.

Believers live in the same world as you, but a believer has a different outlook. We have a present help in times of trouble. The problem may not go away, but we know that if we trust God, He will show us how to fix it, get through it or wait for His solution. We see the same killings, death, sickness, and destruction but we trust that the Sovereign God will protect us THROUGH everything. We know that even in what is happening in this world, He is not surprised by it and has a plan that will work out for the good. Even if we must go through the furnace, we can come out unscathed on this side or end up with Him in Heaven. To us, it is still a victory.

We believe that every day, Christ has given us THE PURPOSE to share His Word with this world. We believe everything we pray and Trust every word of God is sent to guide and lead us. This is our Faith; it helps us through Now, every day, and in every way. It is NOW FAITH.

Hebrews 11:1 Now Faith is the substance of things hoped for and the evidence of things not seen. (NKJV)

Prayer: Lord, this week, my prayer is to get more of you. More belief in you. More Trust in you. More Faith in you. I understand that it takes building up in me. I am ready to be built up. You are the carpenter. You will increase my faith. Show me how to have Now Faith. **AMEN**

Reflection: Expound on places where you stood on faith and places/situations where you can be better next time. Don't kick yourself. We do get better.

Week 4: Allow Time To Heal

We will go through many different experiences throughout our lifetime. Some are good; loves, marriages, births, traveling, playing with your children in the yard. Then there are some bad ones. I need not remind you of the tragedies, losses, or hurts we can endure in such a short lifetime. These bad times have left a few scars. More than we want to count. We walk around feeling rejected, unloved, and unworthy.

I call it internal bleeding. You look alright on the outside but inside you're hemorrhaging.

Just like with physical scarring, you rub on a topical ointment, cocoa butter or something else to heal the skin. You also need to begin to heal those internal scars. Jesus is that internal healing balm we need to rub on our hearts, minds, and attitudes, thus allowing the Holy Spirit to heal us from within.

Healing sometimes hurts. You may have to let go of people who have harmed you, by forgiving them. Forgiveness is for your healing. Letting go is for your healing. Learning to pray for them is your healing. Now once you forgive, take the time to heal. You may need space to do this. Removing them or yourself from the fray temporarily and sometimes permanently could be the answer. Be prayerful about what you should do.

Time will help you not make the same mistakes as before. Choose to be healed from this day forth.

Isaiah 53:5 But he was pierced for our transgressions, He was bruised for our iniquities; The punishment that brought us peace was on Him, and by his stripes we are healed. (NKJV)

Prayer: Father, help me turn my broken heart and shattered mind over to you. Through your stripes, I can be healed. When I am healed, I can be a help to others. Heal me. **AMEN**

Reflection: If the doctor recommends time off from work, we take it. The Great Physician has prescribed time to heal. Lay in His arms and allow His Stripes to be your healing. Yes, you are strong. Even Jesus had to steal away. He would disappear. If the Savior went to get refreshed, why can't you? This week come home and shut down everything. What hurts? List it so Christ can fix it.

Week 5: No Matter What

The Apostle Paul was beaten, stoned, jailed, poisoned, and left for dead. No matter what, he never gave up his hope in the Lord. Once he gave his yes, he never returned to where he came from.

We must be just as determined in our life with Christ. No amount of hurt, betrayal, loss, or anything else, will make us throw in the towel. Most people let go of God's hand when going through traumatic situations.

After losing my father, sister, and 8 other family members passing within a 6-month period; I also lost my job after 20 yrs., amid a pandemic, while fighting the enemy of alcohol addiction in my marriage. I felt like I couldn't fight any harder to keep my mind or my faith. I questioned what I was doing? Wondered if this was worth it?

Let me give you what I gave God, a resounding **YES!** It is worth everything that I have and will go through. I decided at the sudden passing of my sister that I wasn't going to turn away. As I begged God to spare her life, I heard a question in my spirit; If I don't, will you still serve me? It wasn't loud but it was there. If I wasn't committed before, I made up my mind then. As I watched her being unplugged from life support, I gave my answer, "yes Lord." My sister went home to heaven that night. In life, you need to be a **NO MATTER WHAT** child of God.

There will be many hard times. If you are not careful, the residual effects of life can dull your spiritual senses. Remember, Jesus knew what we would go thru and who we would be even before we accepted Him. He still went to the cross and completed the work of Salvation and Eternal Life for you and me. Will you stick with Him?

Job 13:15 Though He slay me, yet will I trust in Him. Even so I will defend my own ways before Him (NKJV)

Prayer: Lord, help me hold on to you no matter what. I know it is easy to fall away. So much in this life is trying to lead me to hell. Bring my mind back to you and your love for me in every situation. Keep my trust in He who can bring me through all things. You have never left me alone. **AMEN**

Reflection: What is trying to push you to the edge? Now flip it and make it a steppingstone.

Week 6: You Are More

You are more than a conqueror, more than an overcomer. More than your past. More than you could ever imagine. You are more through CHRIST. Start letting God's promises take over and defeat the devil. You are loved by the Most High God. The creator of the heavens and earth wants to spend time with you. He cares for you. He wants you to live a life of peace, joy, abundance, and security, and not just when you get to Heaven.

You have to know that Jesus died so that you can be changed. He rose so you can be free. He ascended to complete your salvation and give you a home in heaven. When you start to get down on yourself and not believing you are a special child of God, remind yourself, He came to this earth and died for your sins so that there would be no reason you couldn't survive and fight. He thinks so highly of you that He sent His Son just for you. This is because you are awesome in the eyes of the Lord. Stop beating yourself up for past mistakes. Learn to love yourself like Jesus loves you. You will begin to see yourself as more. Loved More, Blessed More, At Peace More. Believe and receive all in Christ.

You deserve it because the God of everything, the creator of heaven and earth said so. If He thinks you are worth all this, shouldn't you?

After being molested, abused, and beaten by the world, your self-worth can feel low. You need to know that you are worth more to God even if, at that time, you can't see how much MORE you are.

Romans 8:37 "Yet, in all these things we are more than conquerors through Him who loved us (NKJV)

Prayer: Dearest Father of all creation, show me where I am living a defeated life. Give me the wisdom to make the necessary changes so that I can have the life of abundance You describe in Your Word. Help me to know through You, I am MORE. **AMEN**

Reflection: This week, look at ways you knock yourself down. Replace it with affirmations from God.

Week 7: Trying to Get It Right

After praying to be more like Christ, the enemy is going to throw all he has at you. This is an opportunity for God to open us up and show us places where we need to change or be healed.

From the moment you step on this path, there will be tests. Some you will pass easily. Others, not so easy. Those tests that we pass, we celebrate because it could have been worse. Celebration helps us to be motivated to move forward. For those times we missed the mark, we will confess our shortcomings and pray for a better rest of today and improvement in all the tomorrows we have left.

We won't let our trips and slips hold us down. Say this statement daily. *I won't allow me to beat myself up for messing up. Nor will I let the enemy heap accusations of my faults on me. Christ has paid for those things in advance.*

Your power doesn't come from staying down. It comes from getting back up. The only time you have power on your knees is in prayer. Ephesians 6:13 tells us when we have done all we can to stand, keep standing. Every day you wake up, you have the opportunity to get it right again. It is a process, but it can be done.

Start this week by taking control of the little things. Ex. Road rage, complaining and addictions. Work on others as they come up.

Romans 8:1 There is therefore now no condemnation to those who are in Christ Jesus, who do not walk according to the flesh, but according to the Spirit. (NKJV)

Prayer: Father, I pray that every day of my life, I will strive to be the person you want me to be. Help me to get up every time I stumble, reminding me that you are still with me and that I can try again. Thank you for not counting me out. You keep me and help me through all. I will be better because you are with me. Thank you for being with me. **AMEN**

Reflection: This week reflect on how you handled the emotional issues that arose? We will be better each week. List the issue so you can see the triggers. How can you be better?

_____
_____
_____
_____
_____
_____
_____
_____
_____
_____
_____
_____
_____
_____
_____
_____
_____
_____
_____
_____
_____
_____
_____
_____
_____
_____
_____

Week 8: Who Do You Need Me To Be?

As we traverse our way through the days, months, and years, we find ourselves in many different circumstances. Some are emergent, and you need a doctor or police officer. Some are mental, and you need a therapist or counselor. Some may be physical, and you need a spouse or friend.

Whatever the issue, situation or emotion, there is a person, a drug, or an app for that, telling you what you should do, how you should feel, or which way you should go.

Truly no one knows that but God. You want to know which way to go? Go to God in prayer. You want to know if it is right for you? Go to the one who laid the plans in place.

What we seek superficially can't heal, fill or bless you. You still feel broken, hurt, and disturbed when you come home, come down or come back. Instead of seeking outside influences, today let's start seeking the One who knows you and your needs. Go to the one who knows the beat of your heart. He will guide you through all as you allow your issues to rest on Him.

Who do you need Him to be for you today? He is able to take on any of your challenges. He specializes in medicine, family, finances, grief, broken hearts, and minds. He works in all areas of life. Who do you need him to be?

Jehovah Jira –Your Provider; Shalom – your Peace; Raphe - Your Healer.

Matthew 16:15 He said to them," But who do you say that I am?" (NKJV)

Prayer: Father, today I need you to be **(fill in the blank)** in my life. You can do all things but fail. I surrender all to you. I don't want anything else but you. I have put much before my relationship with you. I want all of you and I want to give you all of me. **AMEN**

Reflection: Who did you need HIM to be? Looking over your life, can you see where He has been present even if it was in the background? How did He come through? Keep praying while you are waiting for Him to manifest His blessing.

Week 9: Hand Them Off

Have you been carrying stresses, hurts, guilt and shame for so long that you believe the excess baggage is an appendage?

It is time to let go of that which is not of God. You need to let Jesus sustain you. He will never let you stumble through. He will help you through everything, every day. When the trials of the day try to shackle you down and make you feel weak and broken, you can know that you have a place to drop off those worldly weights. Christ says, "Come to me all who are heavy laden and burdened down." Take the trash to the curb. It stinks.

No more guilt; you couldn't control it. No more shame; you didn't mean it. No more regrets; it wasn't your fault. Give that all to Yeshua. We have a willing receiver. He is ready to take all the hurt, shame, guilt, resentment, rejections, and any other thing you wrestle with off your shoulders. He already took them to the cross. That ended them there. Now, let them go back to the grave where they belong.

Psalm 55:22 Cast your burden on the Lord, And He will sustain you; He shall never permit the righteous to be moved (NKJV)

PRAYER: Today, Father, I give myself away. I let go of anything that I have carried into my today from my yesterdays. I release the regrets that condemn me to a life of imprisonment. I take on your freedoms. I release the shames that have held me captive and estranged from your joy and love. I will walk hand in hand with you because I have let go of the things I carried which kept my hands bound. **AMEN**

Reflection: This week, let's look at things we are carrying that we can't control, change or fix. Realize what is yours and what you picked up along the way. You can't help everyone or save them. Sometimes, the best thing to do is step back and let Jesus work it out.

Week 10: A Friend Indeed

In this life, you need a trusted confidant. That person should be able to step in and take over where you are lacking. They should be with you in the good and the bad times.

As you deal with people, you will notice that in your darkest times, you felt your loneliest. That is because those you called friends were truly associates. Just like the word FRIEND has the word END in it, you will have only a handful that will be with you through to the end. Find one, and be one.

As you learn and grow, you have something to share as well. When you begin to share, you will begin to walk the great commission out and you could walk right into a friendship. Until then, Jesus has promised He will stick closer than a brother. He will be a mother/father, if you need Him. There is only one person that you can truly trust to be there forever. He is a good secret keeper. He is well versed in telling you the truth you need to hear. He is there to lean on and be a shoulder to cry on when you get to the rough sides of this life. He is Jesus.

It can be hard to trust in someone you cannot see, but that is why we as Believers have this thing called Faith. It is in accepting Christ that we learned to believe in Him and now are walking righteously. Though sometimes we stumble we are living a blessed life, one with an expected end.

If you find yourself looking for a friend and you have gotten to the end of your rope, reach for the hem of His garment. You will find the best friend in the world.

John 15:13 Greater love hath no one than to lay down one's life for his friends. (NKJV)

Prayer: Dear God, thank you for being my friend. Help me be a godly friend to those I encounter. I want to show your kind of love to the world. You are a friend to the end. **AMEN**

Reflection: How can you be a better friend? As you look over your week, were there opportunities for you to be that kind of friend? Take note of times you could be better, ways to do so, then do it.

Week 11: Be Still

Have you ever noticed how busy everyone is? From the moment we open our eyes in the morning, we are already organizing, preparing, and racing through our day. Do you know how you want to tell your child to sit down and listen? Well, Father to child, God to HIS baby, that is what He is asking of you.

Do this 2 min. exercise. Find a quiet place and SIT DOWN!

Exercise: Begin to meditate on the Name of Jesus and how you love the Lord. Think about how good He has been to you and nothing else but Jesus. Do this repeatedly. When your mind wanders, start from the beginning until you have completed 2 uninterrupted Jesus minutes.

It seems like this would be easy to do but be honest. Did you have to remind yourself to go back to thinking about Jesus; not dinner, not the kids, the job, or the issues of life. Did you check the time? Just keeping the focus on the Lord can be a task with so much going on. We need to learn to sit still once we have prayed. It is in being still that we can begin to hear **HIS VOICE**. You can't hear from God during all the commotion. It is during **quiet moments** that God speaks to your heart. How can you go where He sends you if you didn't hear where He said to go or what to take with you?

Take time for your Father. He wants to hear from you. Don't forget to be still so you can hear from HIM.

Psalm 46:10 Be still and know that I am God. I will be exalted among the nations; I will be exalted in the earth. (NKJV)

Prayer: Lord, help me to quiet my mind to hear your voice. I want to listen to you. Help me this week, to be determined to set time aside for you. In the AM, at lunch, or before bed, I want to devote my time to you. Build in me your personal prayer room where we can sit down, and you can talk to me. Teach me to run to it and be still. **AMEN**

Reflection: How did you do with the exercise? Try it again this week during lunch or in the shower, extending your time until you give God some uninterrupted time. Did you hear from God? Take note of what you heard.

Week 12: God Has His Eyes On You

If you make your bed in hell or rise up to heaven, God has his eyes on you. Whatever you decide to do, God is watching over you. Because He is with you does not mean He will make you stop doing things that can harm you. He will allow you to make choices.

You don't always learn when you are rescued. It is when we experience life and get to know its ups and downs that we make better choices and follow the purposed paths. That is why the Word says whatever you decide to do, wherever you go, I will keep you. BUT You have a choice to make. God is gently urging us to go down the narrow path. He watches to see if you will take His guidance. He will NOT force you into His Will.

Don't think because you feel like you are in a dark place that God doesn't see your needs. He knows. He is sending little beacons of lights to show you the way out. The lights come in the forms of a friend, a song, His Word or some other route to get your attention. Use what you are given to claw your way back to the top. Don't stay in the darkness. Come out into the marvelous light.

We need you to come out, and we can make this a better place together. God wants to see you walking in His Light. He has His eyes on the most wonderful possession He has, **YOU.**

Psalm 32:8 *I will instruct you and teach you in the way which you should go; I will guide you with my eye. (NKJV)*

Prayer: Dear God, during this week, show me how to see more of you. You are watching me. You keep guard over me. You have never left me. I just don't look for You. Help me to look toward you and walk in your goodness. In walking toward you, I will grow stronger, stand steadfast, and be able to endure till the end. Thank you for keeping up with me. **AMEN**

Reflection: What did you do to better align your life with His direction? Did you notice God watching you? Where are some places you didn't want to take God into with you?

Week 13: The Lessons Are On-Going

As long as we live, we should never stop learning. You may stop going to school after you reach certain degrees, but you should never stop gaining knowledge from our God. He is always showing us new ways, algorithms, and plans for our lives. If you get to the point you can't learn, then you know all that God does. No man knows the mind of the Lord. We can't even fathom the thoughts He has towards us.

Get down off your high place and sit at the feet of the Lord. Here is where we learn how to do it all. He is called Teacher because if you are with Him, you will be learning and growing daily. Paul knew that even with all the power he possessed in the Spiritual realm, his shadow could heal people, he had not arrived by any definition of the word. Paul says not that I have arrived but what I do is press on towards the mark. The mark is when we graduate from this life to our eternal life with Christ. Until we reach the mark, we must keep learning.

We can't be healed until we learn of the sickness within that needs a doctor like Yeshua to teach us His prescription for healing.

You are never so grown or high in prestige or status that God can't teach you something.

Romans 15:4 whatever things were written before were written for our learning, that we through the patience and comfort of the scriptures might have hope. (NKJV)

Prayer: Dear God, show me what you need me to learn today. Give me a thirst for what pleases you. Teach me your ways for my life. Give me sight to see your direction signs in my life and follow the path you have set for me. **AMEN**

Reflection: What have you gone through that you need to learn from this week? Stop the cycle of circles. Don't forget that God has something new to show you today and for all your tomorrows. Call up spiritual reactions to issues that arise.

Week 14: How To Capture Your Thoughts - A, B, C, And Always P

Everyone says get over it or change the way you are going, but how? If you stumble, don't stay down. How do you get up and get back in the fight? Use the A, B, C, and always P method, daily, to help you capture your thoughts.

- **A**lways use the Word. Christ used the Word when the devil came to tempt Him. He always quoted scripture. Remember, you are victorious. You are more than a conqueror. Change what you hear in your head until your good thoughts outweigh the bad.
- **B**elieve and Trust. These go hand-in-hand. You have to believe in Him whose power you come in. Your biological daddy may not have been around. Your Spiritual daddy is the ruler of the world. You must Trust that HE has your best interest in HIS heart and His capable Hands.
- **C**laim the Victory. Walk like it has already happened. Walk in your deliverance until you are fully delivered. I quit smoking cigarettes a year before I became a nonsmoker. I started saying how disgusted I was with the smell of them. I kept saying how much I couldn't stand them. I started throwing them away halfway done. I started stopping. It took me almost a year, but I have been tobacco-free since. I began smoking at 11yrs old. I took it on hard after 18. I was in my 40s when I quit. Just so you know.
  Philippians 4:13 *You can do all things through Christ who strengthens you.* **(NKJV)**
- **P**ray. No matter what we do, it is in prayer that we avail. Sit down and have a conversation with your Savior. Prayer is conversation. Give reverence, pour out your heart, close with thanks and Say Amen. You just prayed. Never stop praying. There is power in prayer.

Reflection: Looking at your week, were there opportunities to believe more in God and not yourself? Did you use your scripture as your weapon against evil thoughts? Where was your prayer?

_____
_____
_____
_____
_____
_____
_____
_____
_____
_____
_____
_____
_____
_____
_____
_____
_____
_____
_____
_____
_____
_____
_____
_____
_____

Week 15: Believe It

As kids you were told to believe in fairytales. Believe in the tooth fairy, Santa Claus and the Easter Bunny. None of which are real. When you were taught about your Lord and Savior, it was because of the lies that you couldn't truly believe in Him. You can't see Him, but He is a true Savior and an able Deliverer. He lived on earth for 33 years so that He could understand what we deal with.

You must believe that He exists. If you can believe in Him, you can believe in yourself to be set free of addiction, hurts, guilts, and anything else. You can believe yourself to be healed. You must believe in what you are praying for and whom you pray to. Even if it has been years, keep praying. Never give up the faith.

The answer doesn't always come in the way you expected or wanted it to appear. You have to look for God to see His Grace. Don't be blind because it doesn't look like what you thought. Maybe you are walking in a place of grief. How do you keep holding on; look for life. Find it in the eyes of a child or in the hand of a friend.

If you believe, there can be more for you in this life. Maybe you think you have already gotten what you are due. Or maybe you say, I don't believe it can get any better than this, or I have been so bad that it must be this way. These are all lies from the enemy.

We must have faith that even if we don't see it now, it can come to pass. We must believe like a child believes in fairytales and have hope for a better tomorrow.

1 Timothy 4:10 "For to this end we both labor and suffer reproach because we trust in the living God, who is the Savior of all men, especially of those who believe" (NKJV)

Prayer: Dear God, this week, teach me to believe in myself and in You. I know You died for me, but I don't walk in full power because I don't submit wholly to you. Teach me to trust in You by showing me what to let go of. I want to be the best image of You. **AMEN**

Fruit From Heaven

Reflection: What things have you been sitting down on in your life? What steps can you take to make it happen? What can you do to trust in God more?

Week 16: Leave A Legacy

We strive to leave an inheritance for our loved ones. We work our entire lives trying to build treasures to pass on when we pass away. We Will away special items, money etc. We give details on how things should be handled. We have placed high value on those things that will waste away. We teach our children to grow material items from that which we gifted.

The bible teaches us to build our treasures in Heaven. God wants us to have nice things. He doesn't want us to desire this world and its things more than we yearn for Him and what He has done for us. The Salvation that has been given and the Eternal Life that is our reward; these are the things we should turn our hearts towards.

Train your children in the way of the Lord, that will last longer than any material thing you can leave them. Giving them the Word of God will give them a foundation to work with when times get hard. Seeing you lean in when the walls are pressing on you gives them perseverance during the storms

If you are going to leave a legacy, give the gift that lasts for generations. It can be passed on without a legal document or court order. Give your family a foundation in Christ. You are walking this thing out. Pass it on to your future generations.

Proverbs 13:22 *A good man leaves an inheritance to his children's children, but the wealth of a sinner is stored up for the righteous.* **(NKJV)**

Prayer: Father, I desire to leave my children's children an inheritance that can sustain them through their lifetime. Help me give them the gift that lasts forever; knowledge and a foundation in you. The only way that will work is if I am walking upright. Keep me in your ways; teach me for the rest of my days. Thank you for the legacy of heavenly riches you have in store for me. **AMEN**

Reflection: How do you want to be remembered? What have you been pouring into the tiny vessel that is your family? It is never too late to change what you are depositing into your treasure pot.

Week 17: I Just Want To Be Saved

Being SAVED isn't hard. It is warding off the fleshly temptations that appear after you have accepted Christ in your life that you should be ready for. If you are asking about it, you are being drawn by the leading of the Holy Spirit. You are ready for something more fulfilling in your life.

The Word says to confess with your mouth and believe with your heart, and you will be saved. Confessing is saying I am a sinner and I need you Jesus in my heart. Believing starts when you trust that Christ came to die and was resurrected for you. Eternal life is the gift. All you have to do is sincerely accept Christ into your heart. Begin to walk in a different direction from what this world is calling you to live or leading you into. It will happen because now you have someone convicting you that the old isn't good for you or it won't be good for you in the long run.

During your journey with the Lord, you will learn how He came to this world and died for our sins, of which we have many. Some you will find out about later as you use this devotional. You will ask for forgiveness then. Trust that it will be a process to be healed from the old you and transformed into the new you. It is HIS Grace that saves us because before you knew Him, He had already come down to this earth and died for your soul. He did this so you could have the gift when you were ready. If you are ready, begin to thank Him for His gift and start your new path today. Blessings to you as you take each step. Don't give up, and don't quit. **You are now SAVED.** Get to a church or at least begin to read the bible and then to a bible teaching venue and start living your best life.

Ephesians 2:8 For by Grace are ye saved through faith; and that not of yourselves: it is the gift of God (NKJV)

Prayer: Dear God, come into my heart and take over my life from this point on. Show me your ways and teach me what I need to do for your kingdom. Thank you for taking me right where I am and making me over. I believe and trust you will never leave or forsake me. I believe you came, died and rose up to save my soul. **AMEN**

Reflection: This week, reflect on the love it took to save you. Note where love saved you from.

Week 18: Always And In All Ways

God is calling for us to keep our minds stayed on Him always. He has given us simple ways of doing this. Here are ways to work through everyday issues.

Always strive: If you put your hand to it, finish out the task, assignment, or duty. Don't give up. If you continue with Jesus, your work will be rewarded. **2Chronicles 15:7 (NKJV)**

Always pray: Talk with Him about everything. He knows all things, but He likes to hear from His children. Like any parent, He wants you to come to him not just in your times of need but always. **1Thessolonians 5:17 (NKJV)**

Always seek Him first: Don't go forward in anything before you check in with Christ. He will keep you safe from harm. Even if you start off and have forgotten to check with Abba Father, return immediately, Seek HIS Guidance, His Will, and His Glory. **Matthew 6:33**

Always live for Him: Give others a visual of who Christ is in you. Especially during the hard times. Then is when it is harder for all to stand, show them how we do it. **Daniel 3:18**

Always Trust: He never leaves or forsakes. When you can't see the outcome, trust the one who wrote the story. All who are with Him are taken care of in His Son's Name. **Hebrews 13:5**

God is calling us to Acknowledge HIM in **all Ways**. Trust Him with our hearts for **always**. Walk with Him in **All Ways** and for **Always.**

Proverbs 3:6 In all your ways acknowledge him, and he shall direct your paths.

Prayer: Lord, help me to keep my mind on you always. I want to walk with you in every way you want me to. I don't want to do what I have been doing. Help me to lean to you constantly in my life. This week, I surrender more of my will to Your WILL. **AMEN**

There are 5 scriptures listed above. Take one a day; meditate and pray.

Fruit From Heaven

Week 19: He Loves Me, He Loves Me Not

Good news, God is not bipolar! When He says He loves you, He means it. There is nothing that you can do or say that will make the Lord of all creation stop loving you. You can run away and get off the grid, you can hide in a cave, you can shake a fist at Him in hurt or turn your back on Him. He will still love you. His love runs deep.

It is us who leave and fall away. There are some who will choose not to accept the Father, and they will miss out on the best gift ever. Not His love, but His salvation. There is a difference between having His Love and having His salvation. His love is unconditional. It is for all men and women regardless of race, color, creed or their love for Him. It is salvation that we miss out on. We mistakenly think we get one with the other. We think if we are good enough, we have His salvation.

Love keeps us on his mind. You are His precious creation. The other gets us in the redemption line as a resident of Heaven, and when you transition from here to eternity, you get rewards and wings; but only if you have accepted Him in your heart.

Stop wrestling with the thought of His Love for you. You are loved. When no one else says they love you, God already has; through Yeshua's work on the cross. When you are feeling alone, you are not because you have the Holy Spirit.

Take hold of the love. Let it sink in. begin to walk in the knowledge of Him who is all-loving and loves you to heaven and beyond.

Romans 8:39 Nor height, nor depth, nor any other created thing, shall be able to separate us from the love of God which is in Christ Jesus our Lord.

Prayer: Heavenly Father, thank you for always loving me. I love you back. Help me to stand in your love confidently. **AMEN**

Reflection: This week, recognize those unloved inner thoughts and replace them with affirmations of God's Love for you. Keep up the good work

Declaration: God loves me. I am victorious. I am fearfully and wonderfully made.

Week 20: Who Loves You Baby?

Back in the 70s, there was a show called Kojak. He was a bald lollipop eating police officer, always coming to the rescue of whomever each week. He was famous for the saying, "Who Loves You Baby?" That was his way of saying you are loved. Don't worry, I got you. I will be there for you. Nowadays, we need to hear this. Especially since we are dealing with so much hate and turmoil in life.

We don't have love for each other like we used to. We are not friendly anymore. People walk around with a chip on their shoulder, just mad. If people could see they are loved, then they might share that love with their brothers, and the world could be a good place to live in. You don't have to wonder about who loves you when you are with God. In fact, He will tell you constantly. He knows all about you, and in spite of that, you are still His chosen vessel.

No matter what you are dealing with, you can rest assured that Your Father cares for you. You are God's most prized creation. He loves you so much that He made a plan for us to share in His eternal love. You can Trust His love will never leave or fail you. He will take care of you.

1 Peter 5:7 Casting all your cares upon him, for he cares for you (NKJV)

Prayer: Dear God, this week, let me see clearly how you are taking care of me and realize you have always been doing that. Even when I didn't know you, you knew me and were directing my steps until I turned up your street. Now I can rest assured that I am yours, and you are with me all the days of my life. Thank you. **AMEN**

Reflection: This week, list ways you can see God's love. If you don't see it, start off with a thought of how He is doing all He can to direct you toward His blessing of eternal life and off the path of hell bound ways we once traveled. He woke you up today to give you another chance to get it right. If that isn't love, what is?

Week 21: The Exchange

Have you ever gone to a swap meet? You have options of things to trade for. In life, we have much we can barter and trade. We can trade our good decisions for bad ones. We can opt to do right instead of wrong. Peace instead of war, LOVE instead of hate. These are choices we can make. We can be good people or hurtful ones.

God wants us to make a choice to walk with Him. When we do, He will exchange your broken heart for His loving one. He will exchange your discouraged mind for one of strength and direction. He will take those hard times and give them a soft landing so you can go forward in your walk instead of sitting down and not moving. Are you ready to let go of the hardships you hold on to? Are you ready to take the hand of Yeshua?

He says come to me all who are heavy ladened and burdened down, and He will give you rest. Let's get to the Father together and let Him swap out all our hurts, heavy loads, and burdened mindsets, exchanging them for a new frame of mind, a new hope, and a path in Christ. The exchange is worth it.

You get the benefits when you turn in that old for God's new.

Matthew 11:28 Come to me, all you who labor and are heavy laden, and I will give you rest. (NKJV)

Prayer: Dear God, thank you for exchanging your life in my place. Because of that, I don't have to be bothered or worried. I know I have to go through life and deal with its ups and downs, but I don't have to let it weigh me down because the battle is not mine. It belongs to you. I accept your help in exchange for my problems. I give it all away so that you can heal, clean, and fix everything.
AMEN

Reflection: What are you tired of carrying? It is time to accept this tradeoff. Give away your burdens and take on His rest. This week, come lay down at the feet of Jesus. When you get up, you will be refreshed.

Week 22: Action Vs. Reaction

A knee-jerk reaction - Someone steps out of bounds, says or does something hurtful, and we react. We go off ranting, cussing, fussing, fighting, and now-a-days killing sprees because of a 2-second reaction.

30 seconds later, the situation is over, has changed, or it was only a misunderstanding. How could I have acted that way, said those things, did what I have done?

We gave way to the emotion and reacted. In doing so, we have lost control and let our ungodly side rule. This is not the way of an overcomer. This is how the enemy works. He uses our emotions and reactions to beat us down.

A knee bent action - When you feel the rise in your attitude, emotional state, or attack mode kicking in - **Stop, Drop and PRAY.**

When I was a kid, this is how they taught us to put out fires Stop, Drop and roll. This is the same way to put out spiritual fires. When negative emotions arise, Stop, Drop, and roll over to your knees.

Pray before you start your day. Pray when you feel the situation going astray. Pray when you get ready to walk away. Pray until you feel your issue fading away. Pray, and the devil must run away. Praying will build up your faith. Put the fire out, **PRAY!**

1 Thessalonians 5:17 Pray without ceasing (NKJV)

Prayer: Father, help me to be aware of my reactions. Let my actions be godlier and not something I will regret later. People don't remember your regrets, only your actions. Help me to act more like you. **AMEN**

Fruit From Heaven

Reflection: How many times did the enemy try and attack? Did you stop and pray? How did your situation change? How will you handle it next time?

Week 23: Renter Or Permanent Resident

Who is "Jesus in your life? Do you call him when you need Him and put Him away when you are through with Him, or do you keep Him close all the time? We treat Jesus like a house guest instead of a permanent resident in our lives. When we are going through trials and tribulations, we invite Him to sleep on the couch and watch us. When we need help, we call Him to bring us out of the lost situation. When we are doing well, we send Him packing until the next time.

A child of God has Jesus in the forefront of their life all the time. We are constantly thinking about him, talking to Him and seeking Him out over all issues and situations. We live, breathe, and have our being in Christ.

If you don't have HIM in front constantly, you will be slipping soon. Something is going to throw you off, and you are going to do something you shouldn't. That might not be big now, but a little yeast spoils the entire loaf. I tell you this from experience. When I am with God and doing my studies, worship, and prayers, though under attack, I usually respond without hesitation as a child of God would. When I am slacking on my communication, studies, and intimate conversations with Jesus is when I am more prone to stumble.

2 Corinthians 13:5 *Examine yourselves as to whether you are in the faith. Test yourselves. Do you not know yourselves, that Jesus Christ is in you? —unless indeed you are disqualified.* **(NKJV)**

Prayer: Lord, I am a work in progress, and you know it. You want my heart. My heart longs for you like a desert that needs water. Help me to come closer to you, willingly. Come live inside me and clear out the wretched ways I have. When I am slacking, help me to reach up. I don't want to succumb to the nature that arises. I want to follow the joy that is you. **AMEN**

Fruit From Heaven

Reflection: This week, look within your heart, see the places where you are lacking in godly ways, ask the Holy Spirit who lives in your heart to show you how to be changed from the inside out.

Week 24: Help My Thoughts

Depending on the simplicity or the complexity of my issues, I would pray and walk away feeling sometimes like the prayer was in vain. When we pray, doubt comes in quickly. You will barely get to AMEN before the promises are stolen. Either we doubted, the enemy came in and stole the possibility/idea or, someone with less faith says that it is impossible. Either way, it is doubt, and it is stealing your FAITH.

Faith comes when you say nothing can stop what God has for me. Faith comes when you say, I can do all things through Christ who strengthens me. Faith comes when you resist the temptation to say I can't or don't do whatever it is I am dreaming of.

We must stop talking ourselves out of the blessings. You do deserve good in your life. Your children deserve health and healing. You deserve a good job, a faithful spouse, or a stronger impact.

When Jesus was asked to heal the boy with demons in Mark 9, the boy's father said, "If You Can?" Jesus replies, IF? As if He were insulted. All that He has done, and there is still doubt. Look at your life. All that HE has done, and you still think He can't. Jesus can do anything. We must believe if it is within HIS WILL, that thing will manifest? Healing is yours; salvation is yours, deliverance from addictions, abuse, or depression is all yours.

The enemy of doubt tried to steal this book many times. He said I couldn't, but I believed in the Lord and pressed my way through this time. You are reading it, so that tells me that God can do all things if you believe.

Mark 9:23 Jesus said to him, "if you can believe, all things are possible to him who believes". (NKJV)

Prayer: Father, Help my unbelief. Let me stand on the tallest of dreams trusting you to manifest them in my life. You said nothing is impossible for you. I am putting more trust in you and less in my abilities and thoughts. You are the creator of all. I know you can take care of me. Thank you for holding me up even when I want to lay down. **AMEN**

Reflection: What are you believing for but because of the size of your dream, you think you can't have it? What do you think about good or bad? Hold on to the good, release the bad to the healing of the Holy Ghost.

Week 25: Thought Catcher

You have heard of the dream catcher. What about the thought catcher? The Word of God says to take captive all ungodly thoughts. We are to recognize and redirect them to the trash bin of our minds. We hang talismans around, which by the way, is not godly, to help us be more peaceful or loving. We use them to remind us of whom we are supposed to be acting like. The problem with that is they have no power. The only thing that can catch thoughts before they set up a festering place is the Word of God. When angry, hurtful thoughts run through your mind, we must fight back with affirmations. Lingering thoughts take a foothold and are hard to evict.

One at a time, you must begin to defend against them. Try it this week on the road rage in your life. When you get ready to cuss, throw up a blessing instead. When that person in line fumbles with their card and you are still waiting, grab that thought of how they should have been ready and say thank you Lord for teaching me your patience today.

The Spiritual Catcher is stronger, but you have to activate it regularly. Also, know the more you try to capture your thoughts, the more things are going to come to set them loose. You just keep capturing them. Even if they squirm and get away sometimes, keep recapturing them.

2 Corinthians 10:5 Casting down arguments and every high thing that exalts itself against the knowledge of God, bringing every thought into captivity to the obedience of Christ (NKJV)

Prayer: Lord, this week, I take captive any thoughts that come to steal my joy and kill my demeanor. I am your child, and that gives me the strength to stand against any thoughts that are not of you in my life. Help me today to remember YOU over my mind's thoughts, and I will be better. Help me not to kick myself when I slip up. Thank you for loving me enough to work with me to capture those wild thoughts. **AMEN.**

Reflection: Track those ugly thoughts you have and conquer them with a blessing from your mouth. Reflect on how your change of thought pattern turned the situation around and how your circumstances and outcome changed.

Week 26: Favor Is Yours

I was once told favor that fell on others was theirs. I couldn't expect that in my life. That thought perplexed me. I have faith in the same God who can do exceedingly and abundantly. What do you mean I can't have it? My Father in Heaven says believe in HIM and ask anything in HIS Name, and it shall be yours if it is within HIS Will for your life.

Don't let anyone tell you that you can't have what you believe for. Then why believe? Christ wants what is best for us. The only way to get that is to have His Favor over us.

Believe knowing that you can have what Christ has designed for you to have. You have the same favor bestowed on those written about in the Bible.

There are things that we will not get because they don't belong to us. Only God knows what you will be blessed with, but keep your Faith, it could be yours tomorrow.

Believe until the doors fall off. You never know when your blessing is coming. What Christ has for you is yours.

We must commit to the Will of God. Begin to walk confidently in His Favor. Wait patiently to receive your blessings.

Psalms 5:12 For you O Lord, will bless the righteous; with favor You will surround him as with a shield.

Prayer: Lord, this week, I open my hands to you. I open them because I had them closed for so long thinking I don't deserve the same blessings as others. **No more!** Your favor is for all your children. It isn't fair on when and whom it will land on, but if I am walking hand in hand with you, I am due favor. I speak Favor into my life, my family, my home, my job, and my pathways in you. Favor is mine because of you. **AMEN**

Reflection: Look over your life, past and present, tell of His Favor. Keep this list close to remind you of all that He has done, and if you made it through this list, you can make it through anything else that comes your way.

Week 27: Which Way Do I Go?

There are many signs on the road to life. It is hard to know which way to go. Take a left here for love. Take a right for prosperity. Make a U-turn up ahead. All this can become confusing.

While driving to Chicago, my GPS called for a right turn. Not at the next corner, but in the next 50 ft., make a right, and it kept saying this repeatedly. The problem was I was over 75 ft in the air on a temporary bridge above where the regular road used to be.

You can't follow every direction given to you by everyone. They don't have all the right information. Our God gives us great directions and instructions in His Word during our journey. If we don't check our compass, we run the risk of getting lost.

The same thing goes when we are traveling down life's Road. If we don't get directions, we can miss our turn. If we don't look at the map, the Bible, how will you know which way to go? You can't listen to people on the side of the road. They are outsiders willing to give directions, but to where? It could be a wrong turn.

You should stop instead, at a well-lit rest stop, your church that teaches the unadulterated truth, a God-fearing companion or on the altar of the Most High in prayer; pull out the road map, allowing the Son to light the way and give direction. You will travel in Peace when you follow His direction.

Matthew 6:33 But seek ye first the kingdom of God and His righteousness, and all these things shall be added unto you. (NKJV)

Prayer: Father in heaven, help me this week to look to you for direction in my life. I have done all I can to lead me, and I have gotten nowhere fast. Now let me allow you to guide my every footstep. You said you would order my steps if only I would allow you to do that. I surrender to you. **AMEN**

Reflection: Did you check your path this week? Where did you allow God to lead? Did you use the GPS? (**G**od's **P**rotective **S**pirit)

Week 28: The Plan Has Already Been Made

It can be hard to recognize you are on a planned path when it seems your life is in an uproar. From every side you are being bombarded with death, health, family, financial, and marital or single-life issues.

When you look up, and you seem to be getting kicked in the head repeatedly, you can wonder if you are on the right path or if God is leading you as you heard. If you are looking toward the hills of heaven, you can be assured that your help and hope are both coming toward you.

It may seem the way is overgrown with debris, but rest assured there is a pathway, and you are on it. Even when you can't see the direction signs, know that you have an inner guiding beacon leading you home. You know the way. It is stamped on your heart.

If you are doing you and not God, then you are off the narrow path and headed toward disaster. It is simple. With God, you are safe. Without Him, you are in danger.

It is **NOT TOO LATE** to return to or come in out of the rain.

Jeremiah 29:11 Msg. I know what I'm doing. I have it all planned out - plans to take care of you, not abandon you, plans to give you the future you hope for

Prayer: Lord, if there is anything that has blinded me from your path for me, reveal it and show me how to release it. I don't want anything between you and me. Let me trust you in all ways. No matter what comes down the road, let me stay on your path. Give me your eyes to see the way. *AMEN*

Reflection: This week let us give our full attention to where we are headed. You cannot change where you have been, but you can change where you are going.

Week 29: Holding My Tongue

I have a good understanding of what holding your tongue looks and feels like. I am a person who doesn't like to shy away when she is riled up. I am being trained to hold my tongue by God. Only He knows what and how to deal with you as He trains you in the way to go.

I know now that the enemy is trying to attack me and my spirituality. This is how the enemy works. He pushes and pokes until you are about to burst at the seams with emotional vulgarities.

God wants us to hold our tongues. This takes a lot of work. It feels like the special words are in my throat, poised to flow out of my mouth with venom attached. They are ready to violate your every being. When suddenly, I feel the Holy Spirit almost choking me, trying to keep me from responding. His Holy Fingers around my throat stopped those hurts from spewing.

Me, wrestling with my emotions and desires, this is how I know I am being changed. The spirit of the Lord has taken up residence. I do not do what I want to do.

When it feels like you are wrestling against something so intensely that you are struggling, almost tussling, that is when you know the Holy Spirit is taking control.

You are resisting, taming, and taking the emotions captive unto the submission of Christ; not you captive to them. There will be resistance; however, the enemy knows he must flee. Hollering and screaming, he still must flee.

James 4:7 Therefore submit to God. Resist the devil, and he will flee from you. (NKJV)

Prayer: Dear God, this week, please help me resist temptations to cuss, fuss or hurt others with my words. Instead, let your words begin to flow from within me. I want to be changed. I give myself away to your healing power. **AMEN**

Reflection: Take note of how you submitted to Yeshua instead of committing the sin of tongue-lashings. How can you be better next week?

Week 30: You're The Plan Maker; God Is The Way Maker

During our journey with God, we will learn that no matter how detail-oriented, how great we throw a party, set up an occasion, or plan a vacation, we cannot plan for the unknown things that might get in the way. Keep in mind; that the best-laid plans can fail due to life's ever-mysterious changes.

The bible tells us God knows the plans He has for us. The plans have already been made. They were written by the finger of God before we were born. This doesn't mean that you don't look forward to blessings, births, weddings, anniversaries, or other happy occasions that come in our tomorrows. You have steps to take and make in this walk.

It does mean, don't spend time fretting over what does or doesn't occur. You can't stop or start anything. You can only live through it, grow during it and find the blessing of God deep within it.

The only way a plan comes to fruition is if we wake up tomorrow, and it is God's Will. We live as if we will wake up on earth tomorrow. We work and love as if tomorrow will come with all we desire. We live for today in the body of God's children, trusting for tomorrow, knowing our forever is in heaven.

As you trust God with your today, go ahead and make plans. They will only open for you by the Way-maker. The Father opens all doors, supplies all help, and gives the uplifting needed or favor poured out to make it happen. Believe in what you know as your plan with a leaning on the way-maker for the path.

Proverbs 16:9 *A man's heart devises his way; but the LORD directs his steps.* **(NKJV)**

Prayer: Father, this week, help me to grab those plans I have made without you and bring them unto the submission of you. If it is your will for them to come to fruition, thank you for your blessing. Show me how to be okay with any plans I have made that are not what you want for me and let them go. I only want the plans you have made and the ways you will open. **AMEN.**

Reflection: What plans are you making? Have you asked God to direct your steps?

Week 31: God Is Working In Your Life

You may think you are not on the right path, or your life is so messed up that God would never do anything for you, but I beg you to look deeper.

Even though you can't see Him. Your God is working things out for your good. It may seem like what is currently happening can't ever work out. It is full of pain, uncertainty and dysfunction but God can change it, heal it and redo the relationship. He can use it for His good.

You will need to recalibrate your vision to see Him working for your good. You will need to recalculate your thinking to take in the new ways you will go and new thoughts you will think. We have been hateful and hurtful or broken and bound for so long; you need new thoughts and a heart transplant to change that behavior.

Our God was raised as a carpenter and He can rebuild and restore all that is broken. Let Him work in your life. You will love the outcome.

Romans 8:28 For we know that all things work together for the good of those that love the Lord and are called according to His purposes.

Prayer: Dear God as you work in my life this week, I will release those things I see need to be changed so you can heal or rebuild me. I give you permission to work on those things I don't know about. Work in the hidden crevices of me so I can be effective in my work for you. **AMEN**

Reflection: Look over where you have been and see how you had to go through some trials so you could end up where God can use you. Do you see steps being laid out for your purpose to flow? What are you going through currently? What have you gone through? How can you use it to grow from instead of drowning in?

Week 32: Sustainable Living

There are many days when we want to give up. If you aren't dealing with something deep now, believe me, you will. I have walked through death with many people. I have lost people in my family, but none affected me the way losing my sister did. I thought I wouldn't breathe again. The gut-punch was powerful. I felt doubled over.

The only way to make it is with a relationship with Christ. The Word tells us many times to cast our burdens on Christ; He will sustain us. When no one else is around, you have a friend in Jesus.

At the time of this writing, I was going through the 1st anniversary of the death of both my father and sister. They died within 2 months, almost to the day of each other. I have never dealt with death as directly as this. This type of grief is different for me, but I have been keeping my mind stayed on Jesus.

He has kept me in perfect peace. He has filled my lungs with His breath, the breath of life. Not that I haven't had emotional upheavals, times of crying that don't seem to end, and anger out of nowhere. All this comes from the grief within, but I have also had Jesus, His Word, and prayer time to help me hold on.

The only way to maintain; coming out victorious is to let Yeshua sustain us. Cast all your burdens on Him. It is in the coming out that you get the victory. It hurts; get up. Those you lost would want you to get up and not wallow in the hurt. The God we serve wants us to get up, stand up and Hold On. You can do it.

Psalm 55:22 Cast your burden on the LORD, And He shall sustain you; He shall never permit the righteous to be moved.

Prayer: Father, You are the Way, the Truth and the Life. With You sustaining us, there is nothing we can't make it through, overcome or break out of. You keep us and remind us that there is nothing You won't do to help us during any trial. We love you and thank you for loving us and being compassionate toward us.
AMEN

Reflection: This week, take note of what you are going through, take a breath, and let Jesus show you how to handle each thing that arises.

Week 33: Will You Truly Believe?

Do you find yourself wondering if God is going to help you? You know He is able but wonder if He is willing? The Father is willing. He believes you can do all things through Him, so He has equipped us for just that. He wants to be there for you during all times, good or bad.

It is easy to believe when you are in the good times of life that God loves you and all is well. It is during the difficulties of life when our faith waivers. When you are faced with a bad health report or you lose your job, can you still trust? When the child gets deeper into trouble than you can help them out of, are you still going to believe? Maybe it is a loss to suicide or murder, will you still believe in the God you served up to this point?

I find myself in the place of believing for provision during a time of lack. I am without a job. I believe God for His books to be my next form of income. I am trusting that I heard the word of God tell me not to get back into the mainstream of work, especially during this mess of Covid19, mandates, and governmental bologna.

I believe in my spirit that if I stand on this written word and His Works, I won't be put to shame. I am believing. If you are reading this, you are a part of the manifestation of God in my life. That is big. He is doing it for me. Now, you need to grasp hold of your dream and put it out there for God to bless. Thank God for this being a working tool in your life, Only God can do that. I believe in you. We can make it.

2 Corinthians 1:20 For all the promises of God are yes and in him Amen, to the glory of God (NKJV).

Prayer: God, where I lack in faith, increase me. Help me to recognize you. You are my God, and I don't want to stray in any way. You are able and have made me ABLE in You. **AMEN**

Reflection: What are you waiting for? Step out in Faith. Take that dream off the shelf. Believe in yourself and especially your God.

Week 34: It's All In Your Mind

The mind is more than a playground for the enemy. It is a full shopping mall, and he gets everything at ½ price. He doesn't have to work hard at using what life has done to us or what we have done in this life. He uses what we have gone through to bring up all these emotions, actions, and pains, knowing we will react in negative ways because we always react badly. We always explode and yell at the kids, the spouse, and the car in front of us. We always drink, smoke, or spend. We are so predictable.

We must choose to actively change our minds. Today is the day we close our mouths and listen to that still small voice telling you, "I have brought you through so much. I will carry you during this time too." God doesn't want us to be stuck in the muddy places of hurt and anger. There you cannot sufficiently protect your family by prayer or fasting. You are bogged down. You are too busy letting the lies overtake you. It stops now.

We overcome by the renewing of our minds, and the only way to do that is to submit to the move of the Holy Spirit. Allow the Holy Spirit to show you the door to new thoughts, thus learning to walk empowered, knowing God's good and perfect will for your life.

It begins by rethinking what you used to do and hearing the Holy Ghost say, now you know that is not right, take this path instead, then following His lead.

Romans 12:2b "be transformed by the renewing of your mind that you may prove what is that good and acceptable and perfect will." **(NKJV)**

Prayer: Lord, change my mind. I have so many old thoughts, and I release those to you. I resist the enemy who is trying to convince me I am not better than I used to be. Thank you for making me over in your image again. *AMEN*

Reflection: Time for a spring cleaning. This week get rid of everything not of God. You know what it is that doesn't feel comfortable, but we do it or hold on to it anyway. Wash off all the dust of yesterday using the Living Water from Heaven.

Week 35: Baby, I Got You Baby!

I used to watch the Sonny and Cher show when I was a kid. They sang this song that simply said, "Babe, I got you babe." This is a great reminder of how our Father feels about us. He is saying to us in His Word that He has us. It doesn't matter where you are, He is with you. He sees us when we are in the right places aligned with His Word. He also knows when we are outside of the Will of God. He tells us that no matter what we do, He is with you.

We need to know; it may get hard to walk this life out. With all the upsets, issues, rejections, shames, and betrayals we face in a lifetime, our God is still with us. He will keep your mind. He is saying if you trust in me, I have your back. If you lean toward me, I will direct your steps. If you follow His commands, He will keep you in perfect peace during any storm. He sings that song to you. Baby, I Got You Baby.

You can stop worrying. You can start trusting and believing. The Father of all creation loves you so much, and He wants you with Him. When you finish with this place we call earth, we have a home with Him in Heaven. Our goal is to get to Heaven. There is only one way, which is through His Son, and finishing the entire journey.

He has done all that it takes to get you to be with Him. You must take the next steps and accept His hand. No matter where you go, He is there. Don't make your bed in hell when you have a heavenly home. He's got you baby.

Psalm 139:10 Even there your hand shall lead me, and your right hand shall hold me. (NKJV)

Prayer: Dear Lord, this week, help me remember that you are with me. You go before me. You make a way for me as I follow your Word. Help me to follow you all my days. You promise to have my back, and I thank you. Thank you for never leaving or forsaking me. **AMEN**

Reflection: Did you recognize God in the places you went? How did that influence where you went and how you acted? Think of times you know it was nobody but God that changed your direction.

Week 36: Let's Get It Started

We start our days with many things; breakfast, phone messages, issues etc. We used to get up early and pray. Then one day, we didn't get up. Instead, we thought, we can pray from our beds. God hears me wherever I am. This is true, He can hear you.

We reason with ourselves every day, staying in bed longer. We talk ourselves out of praying or reading our bibles. Next thing you know, you have skipped so many days that the Son of God becomes secondary. You didn't mean for it to happen, but it has. You still thought about Jesus. You still prayed, but it isn't like it was. You're not waging war like you used to. Your prayers aren't fervent and effectual like they used to be.

At the same time, other things are in your life. You have time to play games on your phone but not read your word? You have time for a spa day or walk in the park but not listen to the bible app on your phone? When was the last time you checked your g-mail (God mail)? Start this day early again. Go back to your standards before you got lackadaisical.

You can't go back in time. You can change the time you have going forward. If you have a feeling you are not spending enough time with Jesus, you probably aren't. Take a few minutes today and give God some of your time. It is the least we can do for all He has done for us.

More time with Him is a solution where everyone benefits. God wins, and You win. You get the rewards of eternal life, peace, joy, hope, and all that comes with knowing Christ. He gets to hear from you, His precious child.

Mark 1:35 Now in the morning, having risen a long while before daylight, He went out and departed to a solitary place, and there He prayed. **(NKJV)**

Prayer: Father, help my communication with you. You are the most important person and I need to get to know you better. Help me stop making excuses about why I can't talk to you. You speak my language. All I need to do is open my mouth and you will hear my heart. **AMEN**

Reflection: Don't just make a To Do list. Get up and do it. This week check something off as completed.

Spent time with Jesus - **CHECK**

Read my bible - **CHECK**

Prayed for my family, friends, job, and this planet - **CHECK**

Week 37: He Never Said A Mumbling Word

Do you talk under your breath or complain? Do you carry an offense and gripe about your situation?

Jesus doesn't want us to complain. He never said a word in complaint. The one person who really could have gone off due to the circumstances never said anything. Could you do that? That is why HE had to be the one to stand in for us. We would have messed it up.

If I were Jesus, I would have struck down those who came against me. I would have said, "I came down from my heavenly home where the throne of my Father is. I walked with the angels, but I chose to come down here for you. You who hate me, curse my name, my laws, and my ways. I came and took the stripes of a thief and death of a murderer. I walked in betrayal and lies. I came and stood in disgrace of a cross. Never did I say a word in hate. You complain of having nothing when your plates run over. You holler about emptiness as though I have not come to fill your whole heart. You whine aloud to anyone who will listen. **BUT, I NEVER SAID A MUMBLING WORD**.

When they beat me for your transgressions, I never said, I don't deserve this. When your sins were heaped on my shoulders, I never cried out, why me? When my Father had to turn away from me while I was covered in your filth, lies and guiltiness, I still held on to complete the work of Salvation.

Take my example to heart. I am the Way, and to go the way I go, you need to become a better image of me.

Starting today, let us look to the bright side. Christ knew after everything was over, you would get salvation and spend eternity with HIM. It made all the suffering worth it.

Philippians 2:14 *Do all things Without complaining and disputing* **(NKJV)**

Prayer: Dear God, this week, make me aware of my grumbling and complaining. Help me to stop and praise your name and raise your standard instead. **AMEN**

Reflection: Did you see places where you would have normally complained and instead, you praised your way through? Each day you are getting better. Keep holding on.

Week 38: Aw Child, Shut Up!

I don't like to tell people to shut up, but I have. There is no reason for this. We can rebuke people with knowledge rather than cut them down with hurtful words.

It is when I was about to act out, or I didn't want to hear another word that someone was speaking, I used this statement. It was to stop the onslaught of lies or what I deemed useless babble. One shouldn't say it. It comes out harsh. SHUT UP!!

That's not how to do it. God is good and loving. He does know that we need to be disciplined or corrected. We need to be shut down or quieted.

I have found a biblical foundation, not the exact wording. **That's right. Our Father has told us to shut up.** God says, be still. That is His way of telling us to stand down, let Him take control, and stop doing what you are doing. It is His way of saying be quiet and sit down. When you have a smart mouth, you need to say it out loud so you can hear yourself. You have to say it when you aren't in the mood, and you want to go off. You have to tell yourself to be still. You also need to say it when you are putting yourself or others down. When you find yourself talking you out of a future or promise you have to tell your mind, the devil's playground, to shut up, to be still.

Proverbs 21:23 Whoever keeps his mouth, and his tongue keeps himself out of trouble. (NKJV)

Dear God, when I open my mouth, and the words about to flow are not of you, remind me to be still. When I am about to say something or do something that will not bring you pleasure or glory, remind me to be still. If I continue to do my will instead of yours, please put your hand over my mouth and tell me to shut up. Hush me and place your Word in me so I can speak life instead of death. **Amen**

Reflection: This week let us be mindful of what we are saying. Tell of the places you heard that Still Small voice urging you to "Be Still."

Week 39: Mind-Changing Power

When you are going through struggles, you have the tendency to overthink and overhear the enemy. He is telling you that you can't be loved or you can't do something, and instead of giving it a try, you say, I can't do that.

You are being told that you can't be worth all that Christ did to bring you salvation. Instead of saying I am worthy, we fall into depression and feel like we are unloved. It can be as drastic as committing suicide because of the lies. If He loved you, why would you go through these things? Truth is, because of our adversary. He brought death into the Garden of Eden. We took it on with the bite of the fruit

Today, let us take captive anything that talks down to us or lies about who God is. Anything that tells us we aren't whom the bible says we are. The scripture tells us we are to demolish these and any arguments that come up against the knowledge of Christ. That is anything that someone has said to you. No matter how many times it was said. If it wasn't in love, it wasn't from Christ, and it won't bring life; throw it away. Change your mind. You are loved. You are powerful.

Let's go out this week and take the day by storm. Find something new and do it. Give more of yourself in projects. You have the skill. If you don't, you will be trained by the Holy Spirit.

2 Corinthians 10:5 Casting down arguments and every high thing that exalts itself against the knowledge of God, bringing every thought into captivity to the obedience of Christ, (NKJV)

Prayer: Lord, every day, I need to have my mind reset. This week Help me to cast away every thought that rises up against you and me. Let me begin to walk in the knowledge of who I am in your sight. You called me victorious, give me the new eyesight to see victory in my life. I am privileged because I am your child. Help me to begin to see my new royal self through you. **AMEN**

Reflection: Write out this week's "Changes Needed Plan" and put it into action.

Week 40: I Believe

Sometimes as you wait on God to manifest that miracle in your life, lack of trust in God and your own self inadequacies rise up in you, causing you to question if God can do all He says He can do. Will He heal me? Will He fix my broken marriage? Will I find my spouse, that job etc.

The enemy would want you to think you can't, it won't, or you don't deserve it. Those are lies that easily beset us because we know who we were in our pasts.

God's word tells us there is nothing impossible for him and we are not who we used to be. **HE is** able to turn the issue around. **HE is** able to bring you out. **HE is** able to heal your body. **HE is** able to change your walk. If it is in His will, **HE is able.**

We must believe with all our heart that God can. This is Faith. Even with that little piece of flesh that says, **"IF,"** we all have been there. That place where we prayed for something and believed for it, but we still have this twinge of doubt that it may not happen. We must still believe.

While waiting on the Lord, don't let disbelief, doubt, or hesitancy creep in. You will miss stepping out if you begin to question the outcome. Faith is moving when you can't see the road ahead, but you know the one who lays the path.

Mark 9:23-24 Jesus said to him if you can believe, all things are possible to him who believes." Immediately the father of the child cried out and said with tears Lord, I believe, help my unbelief. (NKJV)

Prayer: God, forgive my unbelief. I want to believe wholeheartedly; my flesh is weak. I trust you, and you can see past my weakness into the heart of the matter. I need your help to stand in the truth of Faith. Help my unbelief. **AMEN**

Fruit From Heaven

Reflection: What are you waiting for? Go ahead, take a Step. What do you have to gain? Tell about the steps you are taking.

Week 41: It Isn't Getting Any Easier

Look around you. Every day we see violence on TV, hear about it with our youngsters, or have experienced some violent crime in our lifetime. These things are becoming more the normal way of life. This world is not getting any better, and times are not getting easier. This world is becoming exactly as it was described in the book of Timothy.

Since life isn't getting easier, it is vital that we dig deeper into a relationship with Yeshua. It would be easier to get up and walk away, we can't. It is easier to be in this world and do the things of this world, but we have been set apart. Every day we need to try to be better than yesterday. Every day you must fight to be who you are in Christ.

As this world collides with its destiny, shouldn't we strive to be in a steadfast foundational place? It is about to get more real in the world than we could ever have imagined.

These things must come to pass so that we can get to the Rapture. It isn't going to get easier to be of Christ. Are you ready for what it takes to make it? No matter what this world does, are you ready to stand with Christ?

2 Timothy 3:2 For men shall be lovers of their own selves, covetous, boasters, proud, blasphemers, disobedient to parents, unthankful, unholy **(NKJV)**

Prayer Dear God. I see daily how this world is becoming everything you described it as in the last days. Forgive me my trespasses against my neighbor but mainly forgive me what I have done to you. I don't want to be disqualified from my future with you. Help me to long after you more than anything else. Hide me behind your rugged bloody cross so that I am not like this world. Help me to be ok with being different. I pray for this world as it goes through what you have said it would until our great homecoming in heaven. **AMEN**

Reflection: How do you show yourself set apart and in Christ? Think of ways you can rise above your worldly traits.

Week 42: Under Contract

As you walk into your new self, you will encounter many obstacles. Not all are from the heavenly Father to grow you. Some are set up to make you fall by the enemy himself. They are sent to hurt you to the core. Sent to make you give up. The enemy wants to Kill, Steal and Destroy you. He has sent all that he has in his arsenal to bring you down. This is war. Your soul is the prize. He would have you in hell if it were up to him. He is trying to get you before you are sold out to your heavenly residence.

Good News: Someone else is fighting for you and on your behalf. Someone who cares for you. They have put their own contract out on your life. This one came with a down payment. The price that was paid is the highest of all costs. He paid in advance to pull you from the hell you could be in or were headed toward.

We have signed many contracts that don't give all that it promised. Somehow, we missed a clause or sentence, and it made us feel like we were conned. The contract we are under with God doesn't have any hidden language or fees. It is straightforward. If signed, you will not have to fight your own battles. You will have a host of angels to fight on your behalf. This contract secures an eternal resting place and has a retirement plan that is unrivaled.

All you have to do is accept the terms.

TERMS: Believe in Him who came. In exchange, you will receive Eternal Life, Deliverance, Salvation, and Blessings

Revelation 3:20 Behold, I stand at the door and knock: if any man hear my voice, and open the door, I will come into him and dine with Him, and he with Me.

Dear God, let me start this week understanding that you have paid in full with your Holy Life for my eternal soul. Let me recognize if I am out of your will and rectify it immediately. I accept your terms. I want to be in your family. Thank you for fighting for me, waiting for me to read the fine print, and sign with my heart. **AMEN**

Reflection: Note ways you acted outside of the terms of your contract with God and correct that behavior.

_____
_____
_____
_____
_____
_____
_____
_____
_____
_____
_____
_____
_____
_____
_____
_____
_____
_____
_____
_____
_____
_____
_____
_____
_____
_____
_____

Week 43: He Is A Keeper

Our God wants to keep us. He wants to keep us from evil during our hurts and catch us when we are falling. He wants to keep us from hell and damnation. He wants to take care of us so much, that He went through the worst things on earth to bring us to our heavenly home. He was crucified for our transgressions.

As we are waiting for our Savior, we must remain in complete trust that all that has been spoken in our lives spiritually will manifest. You are given many spiritual and material blessings.

For this to work, you have to trust that Our loving God will be keeping you. He will open doors for you. Our God is a promise keeper. He has spoken things into your life, you must believe and work toward His promise.

Don't step in the way of the promise, and especially don't run from it. We step in the way or run from it by talking ourselves out of our purposes and our destinies. Take a class, learn a language, and open yourself up for the promise to manifest. Tell yourself you are victorious. Now take a chance. Begin writing, open that business, start that ministry. **Go for it!**

I found Him to be a keeper, especially in our lives before we got to know who He is. Our God kept us in our dirty and messy places. You could have been dead and gone, but God says it was not yet your time. He keeps us from many consequences that we surely deserve.

Now, what will you do with your second chance?

Psalm 121:5 The LORD is your keeper; the LORD is your shade at your right hand (NKJV)

Prayer: Thank you for sending your Holy Spirit to keep me from the evils I might encounter. Help me know you keep me but not take it for granted because Grace abounds. **AMEN**

Reflection: How has God kept you over your lifetime? It is good to keep up with what you have gone through to see how God has always kept you and know He will continue to do it. We don't wallow in the past. We have survived it. Go ahead, get up. Your God is going to keep you.

Week 44: Free Your Mind - The Rest Will Follow

Over time you've built up a backlog of worldly goo that becomes clogs in your life pipes. They block your happiness and blacken the windows of your heart. You begin to see things in a dull way. Just like roto-rooter clears the drains, so can the Word of God clean out your clogged mindsets.

Every day there are reasons to be broken down from your yesterdays. Look into the face of your tomorrows and be uplifted. There is hope, love, peace, joy, salvation, and deliverance in your tomorrows.

You march forward by releasing the garbage of days gone by. It is when you begin to let go of all that is a weight that your inner spirit will begin to be gladdened. You let go by acknowledging it happened, asking forgiveness, and accepting God has forgiven you. **Now forgive yourself!** Your life begins to change. It is almost automatic that inner good/growth/God will begin to happen.

This doesn't negate the fact that the enemy/life is going to be assaulting you the entire time. This world will try to convince you that you have not overcome, that everyone is against you, especially God, and you don't deserve to live. Let these lies fall to the wayside.

You should know that your God is greater. He has made you strong and able through HIM. You can, and MUST handle things better. In wanting to be better, you may have to encompass the mountain a few times, learning from it, or for many years until you begin to get over it and get your responses cleaned up. If you are willing to allow the new to come in, you can be set free and refreshed. Free your mind. **You are already Free indeed.**

Galatians 5:1 Stand fast therefore in the liberty by which Christ has made us free, and do not be entangled again with a yoke of bondage. (NKJV)

Prayer: Dear God, this week, show me what I hold on to and help me release it to you. Through you, I will be set free. Nothing has a hold on me but you Lord. **AMEN**

Reflection: This week, track what God reveals to you. It may surprise you the things you've held on to. Many hurts may be revealed over time, work through them as God opens your eyes.

Week 45: Overcomer

This world is becoming more and more violent. It is getting harder to go to the store or the movies without wondering if you will come home. The television is a constant reminder of our shortcomings. The Hell in a Hand-basket theory seems to be evolving before our eyes. It is commonplace to hear of multiple shooting deaths in stores, at home, in schools.

Depression is stalking us, hurt is hunting us, and shameful outcomes are skyrocketing amongst our children, the police, and civilians. There is no longer a gang issue. This is a world issue.

As a believer, when we hear or experience life's hardships, we are meant to HOLD ON. We are not to give up. The way may seem bleak, but that is just the view down here. This is a temporary place for us as Spiritual Beings, so don't get too far into what you see. Dig deeper into your Faith. Trust in God. He has a plan for you. If you stay the course, there is nothing you can't make it through, and you will end up in heaven with your loved ones and the Lord.

We have the best image of what it looks like to overcome in Christ who was betrayed, beaten, hung, and died for our sins, and before he died, he still prayed for us to be forgiven. He never stopped loving us. Having risen, He proved that there is a better tomorrow coming if we just keep the faith.

John 16:33b In the world, you will have tribulation. But be of good cheer, I have overcome the world. (NKJV)

Prayer: Dear God, it doesn't matter what I see in this world, I believe with you I can make it through everything. I will keep my faith in you and my eyes toward the hills looking for your help to come to my rescue. I am an overcomer, and I will be victorious. **AMEN**

Reflection: Get up today and let the world know you are still standing. How did you overcome the stresses this week? Don't stop here; keep check of your victories.

Week 46: I Will Be There To Hold Your Hand

I remember as a kid going into a haunted house and being so scared. Thinking that whatever was in there was going to get me and take me to hell. I wasn't alone, but I sure felt like I was. I reached out my hand and grabbed the hand of the person I was with and immediately felt a sense of calm fall on me.

Have you ever been so scared that you wanted to run crying as far away as you could? It is so dark that you felt helpless. In our times of grief, we go through mammoth lonely times. They are enhanced 10x by the thought of the loss. When you lose a job, you feel defeated. When your kids go astray, you feel like a failed parent. When sickness strikes, we worry if we will survive. You want someone to hold your hand, tell you that it will be ok, and walk with you through the storms.

You don't have to fear anything, anymore. We have a protector with us in our scary places. We all have a Savior who came to bring us safely home. He is with us and says He will hold our hands. He was with the 3 Hebrew boys in the furnace, and He will be with you during your furnace times.

While we wait on the move of God to manifest in our lives, we can be assured that the God of All Creation is holding your hand and guiding you through every storm.

Breathe, you've got this. You are not alone.

Isaiah 41:13 For I the Lord your God will hold your right hand, saying to you 'Fear not for I am with you.' (NKJV)

Prayer: Dear Lord, thank you for holding my hand. I don't have to be afraid of anything because you are with me. The shadows of life are easier to face with you by my side. **AMEN**

Reflection: Over this year, you have learned to look for God's hand in your life. Reflect on the ways you have felt safer because you knew you weren't alone. Tell someone how God held your hand. It is time to let someone know what you are experiencing on this new walk with The Lord. Don't be afraid. The Lord is with you.

Week 47: Hope To The Rescue

When you feel like you are constantly on the losing end of life, it makes it difficult to keep going. When you think the world will be better off without you, this is when you need to look in a different direction.

HOPE TO THE RESCUE!

Praying is what we use when we are down, angry, hurting, broken, depressed, or feeling the weight of our world caving in on us. It is in the Words of a Message from God that we get better.

Eternal Hope is best found in Him that is eternal. Temporary hope is found in things of this world, in relationships, family, drugs or alcohol, things we have to hold on to physically. Eternal Hope comes from knowing you have a home outside of earth. You have a Father that loves you. You have a purpose in this life.

Today We resign our life to God's Eternal Hope. It will carry us. It is this HOPE that will hold us up when our weights try to pin us to the ground. It is the crutch we will lean on when the bones of our legs are without strength.

Declaration: I want to lean more on God and less on the world. The World can't give me what God can. It can only leave me broken, sickly, and ashamed.

1 Peter 5:10 But may the God of all grace, who called you to his eternal glory by Christ Jesus, after you have suffered a little while, perfect, establish, strengthen and settle you. (NKJV)

Prayer: Father, forgive my trespasses. I have messed up, again in most cases. I keep trying to do what is right, I find myself here again seeking your forgiveness. Help me to look to your Eternal Hope to sustain me. Where liquor, drugs, sex, food, shopping, or hate have not been able to help, let it be you I look to. There is no devil in this world that will keep me from getting back up. I may have stumbled, but I am reminded you are still the Alpha and Omega. You will catch me with your righteous right hand. You can present me faultless before the Father. Thank you for reminding me that I can make it by your strength and not mine. **AMEN**

Reflection: What Godly choices did you substitute for your worldly responses and actions? How are you doing? Are there places you need to revisit in your healing? It is okay to check yourself for places to improve in your walk.

Week 48: You Have Angels

One day while driving from CO. to IL., I found myself having eaten too much junk and I got sleepy. I needed to pull over, but I thought I could make it past that. I never eat on the road for just this reason. I didn't do what I should. I am also stubborn and prideful. I found this out about me as I let my pride keep me on the highway.

The devil will use Pride to kill you. I blinked longer than I should have at 80 MPH. But Glory to God who has kept me, we didn't have an accident. I looked up, and there was a rest stop coming in 1 mile. I am so glad that the Angels of the Lord were surrounding me in my stupidity. The Lord has given HIS ANGELS CHARGE over you to keep you from messing up His plans for you. He told them to get out there and make a way.

When we do dumb things, they can help us. My help came in the form of a rest stop. I don't recall a sign saying it was coming up, and then it was there. It doesn't matter when or how it got there, I needed it. I could pull off and get some rest. We made it home safely.

You have protection in the form of angels. Though the enemy would rather you die. Your soul is worth nothing to him if you are rooted in Christ. He wants to take your life to break others down whom you would have influenced. Don't do stupid stuff. Pullover. Life is worth nothing if you are not here.

Psalm 91:11 For He shall give His angels charge over you, to keep you in all your ways. (NKJV)

Prayer: Thank you God. I am grateful for your full protective covering in my life. It is because of you that I am here today to bless your name and spread your gospel. Continue to show me my ways that are wrong and could cost me my life so that I can be better and teach others. Thank you for cleaning out pride and stubborn issues in my heart. I will use this in my life daily to grow better in you. **AMEN**

Reflection: Did you notice your angels this week taking care of you? If not, look again.

Week 49: The Offer Is Yours

What God has for you is yours. Salvation, peace, and a new life are yours right now. If you don't take it, the offer doesn't expire. It does have a due date. This gift is yours up until the very last breath in your body. Then it will be gone. Here is the dilemma, you don't know when your last breath will be. You could die from a long-term illness, knowing a possible date of death, OR you could go outside, get into an accident or have a heart attack and be taken out immediately. You don't want to wait until the last call. You might not get a chance to repent before you die.

 An offer has been made, will you choose to live in Christ or die in damnation. If you choose to live, when will you take the offer? We tend to procrastinate. We straddle the fence. We want to be on the Godly side of life, but just in case it isn't all that we think it should be, we stand with our foot in the worldly things.

Choose today whom you will serve. We plan for children, vacations, retirement, and funerals. Is there no arrangement for God in your life? The Son of God came to save that which was lost. Don't you want to be assured of your final destination?

Isaiah 55:6 Seek the LORD while He may be found, Call upon Him while He is near. (NKJV)

Prayer: Dear God, I accept the offer of you in my life. I no longer want to do this without you. I don't want to wait until the last minute because I might not get the chance to say "Yes." Take my heart now. Forgive my sins. Show me your ways that I might walk in your blessed assurance. Thank you for everything you have done to bring me to your gift of salvation. **AMEN**

Reflection: What took place this week that you may not have survived? Now that you are here today, will you take the offer? If yes, welcome home. If not yet, why?

Week 50: The Gift That Keeps On Giving

I don't celebrate Christmas anymore. With all the stress, depression, and anxiety associated with it, I find it to be less than enjoyable. In my studies, I didn't even find a biblical account of Christmas. It makes it easy not to participate when you don't have a basis for the lie to live in your life. Not that I stop anyone from celebrating what they believe in. What I do celebrate is Yeshua, Our God, His Life, and the blessings that came from it.

He has given you a gift that won't cause you to overspend financially. He has given the gift that won't fall apart after years of use. This gift is solid and sturdy. It is stable in all weather conditions. It is the gift of salvation that comes with so many useful features. In salvation, you can have peace that surpasses understanding. This is achieved when you open up the Word of God. In your peace, you can find unconditional love. After all, what have you to hate on when you find out how loved you truly are? In your love, you can find HOPE, hope for tomorrow. Even in the worst pain, there is always hope for a bright new next day.

This year my gifts are more tangible than ever because they touch my heart and reach out to you. Take what is being given. Today you are given the gift that keeps on giving, Christ.

2 Corinthians 9:15 *Thanks be to God for His indescribable gift.* **(NKJV)**

Prayer: Dear God, thank you for your forever gift. You have done so much for me. I am glad you love me. Your gift of your Son to save me is indescribably the best thing that has ever happened to me. Help me give back without tiring so that others will be led to you through my life. Teach me to appreciate every piece of who You are in my life. I want to cherish all through you. I love you. Thank You in Jesus Name. **Amen.**

Reflection: How do you recognize God's gift in your life? This week lists ways to be a gift to someone, then be it. Keep it simple to start. Don't take on too much. Pray about it.

Week 51: Clean My Heart

As we end the devotional year, reflect on the past days and months. What was good? What can I let go of? We look for things that are cluttered in our homes, and we throw them out. The same concept can be used in your spiritual life. Every now and then, we need to take a dust mop to the cobwebs of our lives. It is time to take the word of God and get into those tight places where dirt hides. It hides in our minds, our hearts, and in those sugary words that are spoken with internal disdain.

You don't want to be heavy as you go into your new beginning. You want to release the past so you can be fresh for tomorrow. That's right. Tomorrow is coming with all its glory, unless God says differently. There will be good times and sadness. Therefore, we should not worry about tomorrow. When it gets here, it will have enough troubles of its own, and we don't want to give it more because we never released the burdens we carried.

Today I ask the Lord to give us a clean heart. To break our hearts to what breaks HIS. To change our minds and thoughts so that we begin to love and spread hope. That is what we are getting from God.

Now we can invite and direct sinners' home. As well, we can get better and stronger individually. That is the goal. Every day we get less bitter and a whole lot better.

Psalm 51:10 Create in me a pure heart, O God, and renew a steadfast spirit within me (NKJV)

Prayer: God, thank you for changing my heart. Continue to work through any residual bitterness and hurt I might carry. I am looking toward a brighter future in you. I understand it won't be easy, but it is possible. Help me accept all your cleansing Holy Spirit does to wash me thoroughly. Continue to show me how to use your Word in my life to keep the dirt from returning. I will dust my heart off regularly with your love and power. Help me to use the cleansing tools you have given. **AMEN.**

Reflection: Meditate on how you have been being changed, challenged and grown. Share your growth and the steps God used to help you. This is an active journal. Activate someone else.

_____
_____
_____
_____
_____
_____
_____
_____
_____
_____
_____
_____
_____
_____
_____
_____
_____
_____
_____
_____
_____
_____
_____
_____
_____
_____
_____
_____

Week 52: It Is Finished

Have you ever wondered what Christ meant when He said these last words on the cross? It means you are finished waiting on a Savior; He has come. You are through dealing with life on your own; you have a friend in Jesus. It means that even in the darkest of days or direst of situations, your God will never leave or forsake you. It means you are not a weakling; you are strong in Jesus.

After everything I went through, I needed to hear this. I needed to understand that nothing can separate me from the Love which is God and the love HE has for me. Not one of my thoughts, hurting times, or slipups can discount me. Not anything I have done that I have asked to be forgiven for, can keep me from being with Our Father in the end times. The sins that I am sure to commit in the future won't keep me away either.

He has promised that as long as you are with Him, keeping your mind stayed on Him, striving to be righteous in Him, He will keep you not just in His perfect peace. He will keep you in all ways if you just TRUST Him.

This means that as you walk with God, He is forever with you. Don't worry, we will slip up. God promised to be there to pick us up as long as we keep looking up.

Your worrying is finished. Your salvation is finished by the work on the cross. Your future is written in Christ as you live in Him. It is Finished!!

John 19:30 When he had received the drink, Jesus said, "It is finished."

Prayer: Dear God, I release any old baggage from years past. Forgive me and help me to forgive those who have hurt me. Lead me into my next year, so I don't pick up any excess baggage. This coming year will have enough of its own, and I don't need to bring extra for the journey. **AMEN**

Reflection: As we wrap up this devotional, what can you let go of? What have you been saving that you no longer need because it is dead weight? Let's look through the closets of our lives and see what doesn't fit and throw it away. It is finished. Use these last pages to list things you need to work on in your new year. We throw out leftovers when they get old. Let's start the next year feeling lighter in spirit.

The Final Word

Praise God, you have just spent 1 year meditating on the Word of God and testing it in your life. Our Father is well pleased with you. Your relationship with Christ has grown. You are not who you used to be. You are dealing with upheaval and unrest with a new sense of who you are and whose you are.

Don't let the enemy come in now and tell you that you aren't making strides. I know if you work on your relationship with God, He will not let you be put to shame. He loves to show up in His believers' lives. Trust Him and Trust His Process.

Remember, He watches over His Word to perform it in your life **(Jeremiah 1:12)**. He is not a man that He should lie **(Numbers 23:19)**, so if you believe and hold on to His Righteous Hand, there is nothing you can't make it through, He promises.

Let me reiterate that you will go through hard times. Look at the Apostle Paul's life to know that salvation doesn't get you out of persecution. If Christ was persecuted, just know you will go through it too.

Since all of God's Word is true, everything must occur, including the end of times. I pray this devotional has shown you that being on this side with Jesus is better than being lost and without hope.

Now you can walk away from here and go the other way, that is your free will. We all have to choose (Joshua 24:15). The Father has reached out His Hand to you. Will you continue to sink or reach up and live?

We all want to make it in this life the best way we can. The best way to survive this world is with a Rock named Jesus as your foundation. He is the Way, the Truth, and the Life.

God Bless you. Thank you from the bottom of my heart. Remember, if nobody tells you they love you, let me say, I LOVE YOU. But know this without a shadow of a doubt, God loves you so much more. **(John 3:16)**

Made in the USA
Columbia, SC
06 January 2023

bf4394f0-8e90-45b4-8ba2-b0e29b473563R05